Congressional
Research Service
Informing the legislative debate since 1914 _____

Congressional Liaison Offices of Selected Federal Agencies

Audrey Celeste Crane-Hirsch
Information Research Specialist

January 7, 2014

Congressional Research Service

7-5700

www.crs.gov

98-446

Summary

This list of about 200 congressional liaison offices is intended to help congressional offices in placing telephone calls and addressing correspondence to government agencies. In each case, the information was supplied by the agency itself and is current as of the date of publication. Entries are arranged alphabetically in four sections: legislative branch; judicial branch; executive branch; and agencies, boards, and commissions.

Specific telephone numbers for correspondence, publications, and fax transmissions have been provided for each applicable agency. When using fax, it is important to include the entire mailing address on a cover sheet, as many of the listed fax machines are not directly located in the liaison offices.

A number of agency listings include an e-mail address. When e-mailing agencies please remember to include your name, affiliation, phone number, and return address, to ensure a speedy response. Users should be aware that e-mail is not a confidential means of transmission.

This report was produced for congressional offices only. It will be updated frequently.

CONGRESSIONAL OFFICE USE ONLY

Contents

Contacts

Legislative Branch

Congressional Budget Office

Edward "Sandy" Davis
Associate Director for Legislative Affairs
Congressional Budget Office
Ford House Office Building
Second and D Streets, SW, Room 402
Washington, DC 20515

Tel: (202) 226-2700
Publications: (202) 226-2809
Fax: (202) 225-7509
E-mail: sandyd@cbo.gov
http://www.cbo.gov

Government Accountability Office

Katherine "Kate" Siggerud
Managing Director, Office of Congressional
Relations
Government Accountability Office
441 G Street, NW, Room 7125
Washington, DC 20548

Tel: (202) 512-4400
Publications: (202) 512-6000
Fax: (202) 512-7919, -4641
http://www.gao.gov/

Until July 2004, this agency was known as the General Accounting Office.

Government Printing Office

Lyle Green
Managing Director, Official Journals of Government
U.S. Government Printing Office
732 North Capitol Street, NW, Room C-730
Washington, DC 20401

Tel: (202) 512-0224
Fax: (202) 512-1101
E-mail: llgreen@gpo.gov
http://www.gpo.gov/congressional/

Andrew M. Sherman
Chief of Staff
U.S. Government Printing Office
732 North Capitol Street, NW, Room C-804
Washington, DC 20401

Tel: (202) 512-1991
Fax: (202) 512-1293
E-mail: asherman@gpo.gov

Mary Alice Baish
Superintendent of Documents
Sales program order desk

Tel: (202) 512-1313
mabaish@gpo.gov

Public Orders: (202) 512-1800 or toll-free
1-866-512-1800 outside 202 area code
Fax: (202) 512-2250
Fax orders (requires GPO Deposit
Account or a Discover, Mastercard, or
Visa credit card)

Library of Congress

Kathleen Ott
Director, Congressional Relations Office
Library of Congress
101 Independence Avenue, SE
Washington, DC 20540-1030

Capitol ext. 7-6577
Tel: (202) 707-6577
Fax: (202) 707-4350
http://www.loc.gov/lcnet/

Loan Division (requests for books): Capitol ext. 7-5445
Tel: (202) 707-5445
Fax: (202) 707-5986

Congressional Research Service

Mary Mazanec Capitol ext. 7-5700
Director Tel: (202) 707-5700
Congressional Research Service Fax: (202) 707-6745
Library of Congress http://www.crs.gov
101 Independence Avenue, SE
Washington, DC 20540-7210

Judicial Branch

Supreme Court

Kathy Arberg Tel: (202) 479-3211 (press 1)
Public Information Officer Fax: (202) 479-3388
Supreme Court of the United States http://www.supremecourtus.gov
One First Street, NE
Washington, DC 20543

U.S. Courts

Cordia A. Strom Tel: (202) 502-1700
Assistant Director for Legislative Affairs Fax: (202)502-1799
Office of Legislative Affairs http://www.uscourts.gov
Administrative Office of the United States Courts
Thurgood Marshall Federal Judiciary Building
One Columbus Circle, NE, Suite 7-110
Washington, DC 20544

The Administrative Office represents all federal courts in interaction with Congress.

Tax Court

Clerk of Court's Office Tel: (202) 521-4600 (must dial 202)
United States Tax Court http://www.ustaxcourt.gov
400 Second Street, NW
Washington, DC 20217-0002

Executive Branch

Executive Office of the President

The White House

Robert Nabors
Assistant to the President for Legislative Affairs
The White House
West Wing
1600 Pennsylvania Avenue, NW
Washington, DC 20502

Tel: (202) 456-2230
Fax: (202) 456-1573
http://www.whitehouse.gov/

For House offices:
Jon Samuels
Deputy Assistant to the President
for Legislative Affairs—House
East Wing

Tel: (202) 456-6620
Fax: (202) 456-1573

For Senate offices:
Jules Edward "Ed" Pagano
Deputy Assistant to the President for Legislative
Affairs—Senate East Wing

Tel: (202) 456-6493
Fax: (202) 456-6468

Office of the First Lady

Melissa Winter
Deputy Chief of Staff
Office of the First Lady
The White House
1600 Pennsylvania Avenue, NW
Washington, DC 20500

Tel: (202) 456-7064
Fax: (202) 456-2237

Council of Economic Advisers

Jessica Schumer
Chief of Staff
Council of Economic Advisers
725 17th Street, NW
Washington, DC 20502

Tel: (202) 395-5084
Fax: (202) 456-3080
E-mail: jschumer@cea.eop.gov
http://www.whitehouse.gov/cea/

Council on Environmental Quality

Trent Bauserman
Associate Director for Legislative Affairs
Council on Environmental Quality
730 Jackson Place, NW
Washington, DC 20503

Tel: (202) 395-5750
Fax: (202) 456-6546
http://www.whitehouse.gov/ceq/

Homeland Security Council

White House Legislative Affairs
Eisenhower Executive Office Building, Room 212
1650 Pennsylvania Avenue, NW
Washington, DC 20502

Tel: (202) 456-2230
Fax: (202) 456-6915

National Security Council

Greta Lundeberg
Senior Director for Legislative Affairs
National Security Council
Eisenhower Executive Office Building, Room 307
1650 Pennsylvania Avenue, NW
Washington, DC 20504

Tel: (202) 456-9171

http://www.whitehouse.gov/nsc/
index.html

Office of Management and Budget

Kristen Sarri
Associate Director for Legislative Affairs
Eisenhower Executive Office Building, Room 251
1650 Pennsylvania Avenue, NW
Washington, DC 20503

Tel: (202) 395-4790
Fax: (202) 395-3729
http://www.whitehouse.gov/omb/

Office of National Drug Control Policy

Kimberly Alton
Associate Director for Legislative Affairs
Office of National Drug Control Policy
750 Seventeenth Street, NW
Washington, DC 20503

Tel: (202) 395-6602
Fax: (202) 395-6640
E-mail: kalton@ondcp.eop.gov
http://www.whitehouse.gov/ondcp

Office of Science and Technology Policy

Donna Pignatelli
Assistant Director for Legislative Affairs
Office of Science and Technology Policy
Eisenhower Executive Office Building
1650 Pennsylvania Avenue, NW
Washington, DC 20502

Tel: (202) 456-7116
Fax: (202) 456-6021
E-mail: dpignatelli@ostp.eop.gov
http://www.ostp.gov/

Office of the U.S. Trade Representative

René Muñoz
Acting Assistant U.S. Trade Representative for
Congressional Affairs
600 Seventeenth Street, NW
Washington, DC 20508

Tel: (202) 395-6951
Fax: (202) 395-4656
http://www.ustr.gov/

Office of the Vice President

Tonya Williams
Director of Legislative Affairs
Office of the Vice President
Room S-212, The Capitol
Washington, DC 20510

Capitol ext. 4-2424
Tel: (202) 224-2424
Fax: (202) 228-1475

Departments

Department of Agriculture

Brian Baenig
Assistant Secretary for Congressional Relations
U.S. Department of Agriculture
219A Whitten Building
1400 Independence Avenue, SW
Washington, DC 20250

Tel: (202) 720-7095
Fax: (202) 720-8077
http://www.usda.gov/wps/portal/usdahome

Forest Service

Douglas Crandall
Director, Legislative Affairs Staff
U.S. Department of Agriculture
Yates Building, 5th Floor, NW Wing
201 Fourteenth Street, SW
Washington, DC 20250

Tel: (202) 205-1637
Fax: (202) 205-1225
http://www.fs.fed.us/

Department of Commerce

Margaret Cummisky
Assistant Secretary of Legislative and Intergovernmental Affairs
U.S. Department of Commerce
Room 5421
Fourteenth Street and Constitution Avenue, NW
Washington, DC 20230

Tel: (202) 482-3663
Fax: (202) 482-4420
http://www.commerce.gov

Economic Development Administration

Angela Ewell-Madison
Director of Legislative and Intergovernmental Affairs
Economic Development Administration
U.S. Department of Commerce
Herbert Hoover Building, Room 71015
Fourteenth Street and Constitution Avenue, NW
Washington, DC 20230

Tel: (202) 482-2900
Fax: (202) 482-2838
http://www.eda.gov/

International Trade Administration

Jordan Haas
Director, Office of Legislative and Intergovernmental Affairs
International Trade Administration
U.S. Department of Commerce
Herbert Hoover Building, Room 3424
Fourteenth Street and Constitution Avenue, NW
Washington, DC 20230

Tel: (202) 482-3015
http://trade.gov/index.asp

Minority Business Development Agency

Kimberly Marcus
Associate Director of Office of Legislative, Education, and
Intergovernmental Affairs
U.S. Department of Commerce
Herbert Hoover Building, Room 5061
Fourteenth Street and Constitution Avenue, NW
Washington, DC 20230

Tel: (202) 482-6272
Fax: (202) 482-2562
http://www.mbda.gov/

National Institute of Standards and Technology

Jim Schufreider
Director, Office of Congressional and Legislative Affairs
National Institute of Standards and Technology
U.S. Department of Commerce
100 Bureau Drive
Gaithersburg, MD 20899-1002

Tel: (301) 975-3080
Fax: (301) 869-8972
E-mail: jim.schufreider@nist.gov
http://www.nist.gov/

National Oceanic and Atmospheric Administration

Amanda Hallberg Greenwell
Director, Office of Legislative and Intergovernmental Affairs
National Oceanic and Atmospheric Administration
U.S. Department of Commerce
Herbert Hoover Building, Room A100
1401 Constitution Avenue, NW
Washington, DC 20230

Tel: (202) 482-4981
Fax: (202) 482-4960
http://www.noaa.gov/
http://www.legislative.noaa.gov/

National Telecommunications and Information Administration

Jim Wasilewski
Director for Congressional Affairs
National Telecommunications and Information Administration
U.S. Department of Commerce
Herbert Hoover Building, Room 4898
Fourteenth Street and Constitution Avenue, NW
Washington, DC 20230

Tel: (202) 482-1551
Fax: (202) 501-0536
E-mail: jwasilewski@ntia.doc.gov
http://www.ntia.doc.gov/

Patent and Trademark Office

Dana Robert Colarulli
Director, Office of Governmental Affairs
U.S. Patent and Trademark Office
P.O. Box 1450
Madison Building, 10th Floor West
600 Dulaney Street
Alexandria, VA 22313-1450

Tel: (571) 272-7300
Fax: (571) 273-0085
E-mail: dana.colarulli@uspto.gov
http://www.uspto.gov/

U.S. Census Bureau

Angela M. Manso
Chief of Congressional Affairs
U.S. Department of Commerce
U.S. Census Bureau
Washington, DC 20233

Tel: (301) 763-6100
Fax: (301) 763-3780
E-mail: cao@census.gov
http://www.census.gov/

Department of Defense

Elizabeth King
Assistant Secretary of Defense
for Legislative Affairs
U.S. Department of Defense
1300 Defense Pentagon
Washington, DC 20301-1300

Tel: (703) 697-6210
Tel: (571) 256-8111 (case-related matters)
Fax: (703) 693-5530
http://www.defenselink.mil

Defense Intelligence Agency

Cal Temple
Director, Corporate Communications
Defense Intelligence Agency
ATTN: CP
200 MacDill Boulevard
Joint Base Anacostia-Bolling
Washington, DC 20340

Tel: (202) 231-0800
Fax: (202) 231-0851
http://www.dia.mil/

Defense Logistics Agency

Robert (Bob) Wimple, USAF (Retired)
Director, Legislative Affairs
Defense Logistics Agency
Department of Defense
8725 John J. Kingman Road
Fort Belvoir, VA 22060-6221

Tel: (703) 767-5264
Fax: (703) 767-6312
http://www.dla.mil/

Defense Security Cooperation Agency

Vanessa Murray
Director, Legislative and Public Affairs Office
Defense Security Cooperation Agency
Department of Defense
2800 Defense Pentagon
Washington, DC 20301-2800

Tel: (703) 604-6617
http://www.dsca.mil/
E-mail: vanessa.murray@dsca.mil
E-mail: LPA-web@dsca.mil

Senate Liaison:
Lorna Jons

Tel: (703) 604-6618
E-mail: lorna.jons@dsca.mil

House Liaison:
Neil Hedlund

Tel: (703) 604-6621
E-mail: neil.hedlund@dsca.mil

Responsible **only** for military-military cooperation with allies worldwide. Security clearances are handled by the Defense Security Service, below.

Defense Security Service

Jon Bennett
Congressional Liaison
2331 Mill Road
Alexandria, VA 22314

Tel: (703) 617-2352
Fax: (703) 325-6545
http://www.dss.mil

Oversees the protection of national security assets and provides integrated security services to the Department of Defense.

Department of the Air Force

Maj. Gen. Tod Wolters
Director of Legislative Liaison
Secretary of Air Force/Office of Legislative Liaison
U.S. Department of the Air Force
1160 Air Force Pentagon
Washington, DC 20330-1160

Tel: (703) 697-8153
Fax: (703) 697-2001
http://www.af.mil

Correspondence/Casework:

Col. Stephen T. Carson
Chief, Office of Congressional Affairs
1160 Air Force Pentagon
Washington, DC 20330-1660

Tel: (703) 695-7364
Fax: (703) 693-6340
E-mail: saflli.workflow@pentagon.af.mil

For House offices:

Col. Patrick McKenzie
Chief, House Liaison Division
B-322 Rayburn House Office Building
U.S. House of Representatives
Washington, DC 20515

Capitol ext. 5-6656
Tel: (202) 225-6656
Fax: (202) 685-2592

For Senate offices:

Col. Billy Thompson
Chief, Senate Liaison Division
182 Russell Senate Office Building
U.S. Senate
Washington, DC 20510

Capitol ext. 4-2481
Tel: (202) 224-2481
Fax: (202) 685-2575

Department of the Army

Maj. Gen. William E. Rapp
Chief of Army Legislative Liaison
U.S. Department of the Army
1600 Army Pentagon
Washington, DC 20310-1600

Tel: (703) 697-6767
Fax: (703) 693-4942
http://ocll.hqda.pentagon.mil/

Tony Adams, Team Chief, (703) 614-9582
Requests regarding:
AL, AK, AR, AZ, CA, CO, HI, IA, ID, IL, IN, KS, LA, MN, MO, MT, ND, NE, NM, NV, OH, OK, OR, SD, TX, UT,
WA, WI, and WY
Ms. Carol Robinson, Team Chief, (703) 697-9687
Requests regarding:
AS, CT, DC, DE, FL, GA, GU, KY, MA, MD, ME, MI, MS, NC, NH, NJ, NY, PA, PR, RI, SC, TN, VT, VA, VI, and WV

For House offices:

Col. La'Tonya Lynn
B-325 Rayburn House Office Building
U.S. House of Representatives
Washington, DC 20515

Tel: (202) 685-2676
Fax: (202) 685-2674

For Senate offices:

Col. Robert McAleer
183 Russell Senate Office Building
U.S. Senate
Washington, DC 20510

Capitol ext. 4-2881
Tel: (202) 224-2881
Fax: (703) 693-4754

U.S. Army Corps of Engineers

Jennifer Greer
Congressional Affairs Officer
U.S. Army Corps of Engineers (CECS-C)
Government Accountability Office Building
441 G Street, NW, Attn: CECS-C
Washington, DC 20314

Tel: (202) 761-4113
Fax: (202) 761-4370
http://www.usace.army.mil/

Department of the Navy

Rear Admiral Mike Franken
Chief of Legislative Affairs
Department of the Navy
1300 Navy Pentagon
Washington, DC 20350-1300

Tel: (703) 697-7146
Fax: (703) 697-1009
http://www.navy.mil/

For House offices:

CAPT Andy Whitson
Director, House Liaison Office
Department of the Navy
B-324 Rayburn House Office Building
U.S. House of Representatives
Washington, DC 20515

Tel: (202) 225-7126
Fax: (202) 685-6077

For Senate offices:

CAPT Cedric Pringle
Director, Senate Liaison Office
Department of the Navy
182 Russell Senate Office Building
U.S. Senate
Washington, DC 20510

Tel: (202) 224-4682
Fax: (202) 685-6005

U.S. Marine Corps

Office of Legislative Affairs

Tel: (703) 614-1686
Correspondence: (703) 614-1738
Fax: (703) 614-4172

For House offices:

Col. Select Daniel Greenwood
Director, House Liaison Office
B-324 Rayburn House Office Building
U.S. House of Representatives
Washington, DC 20515

Tel: (202) 225-7124
Fax: (703) 614-4172 (case-related matters)
http://www.marines.mil/unit/hqmc/Pages/
default.aspx

For Senate offices:

Col. Robert W. Jones
Director, Senate Liaison Office
182 Russell Senate Office Building
U.S. Senate
Washington, DC 20510

Tel: (202) 224-4681
Fax: (202) 685-6005

Joint Chiefs of Staff

Col. Jenny Davis
Legislative Assistant
Joint Chiefs of Staff
The Pentagon, Room 2D920
Washington, DC 20318-9999

Tel: (703) 614-1777
Fax: (703) 697-3083
http://www.jcs.mil/

National Geospatial-Intelligence Agency (NGA)

Christine Monaco
Director of Congressional Affairs
National Geospatial-Intelligence Agency
7500 Geoint Drive
Springfield, VA 22150

Tel: (571) 557-5300
Fax (unclassified): (571) 558-3216
Fax (secure): (571) 558-0989
https://www1.nga.mil/

National Security Agency/Central Security Service

Ethan L. Bauman
Director, Legislative Affairs Office
National Security Agency/Central Security Service
Department of Defense, Suite 6282
Ft. George Meade, MD 20755

Tel: (301) 688-7246
Fax: (443) 634-2274
http://www.nsa.gov/

Department of Education

Gabriella Gomez
Assistant Secretary for Legislative and Congressional Affairs
U.S. Department of Education
400 Maryland Avenue, SW
Washington, DC 20202-3100

Tel: (202) 401-0020
Fax: (202) 401-1438
http://www.ed.gov/index.jhtml

Office for Civil Rights

Russlynn Ali
Assistant Secretary for the Office for Civil Rights
U.S. Department of Education
400 Maryland Avenue, SW
Washington, DC 20202-1100

Tel: (202) 453-5900
Fax: (202) 453-6010
http://www.ed.gov/about/offices/list/ocr/
index.html?src=mr

Department of Energy

Brad Crowell
Assistant Secretary for Congressional and
Intergovernmental Affairs
U.S. Department of Energy
Forrestal Building, Room 7B138
1000 Independence Avenue, SW
Washington, DC 20585-0800

Tel: (202) 586-5450
Fax: (202) 586-4891
http://www.energy.gov/nationalsecurity/
index.htm

Federal Energy Regulatory Commission

Chris Murray
Director, Division of Governmental Affairs
Federal Energy Regulatory Commission
888 First Street, NE, Room 11H
Washington, DC 20426

Tel: (202) 502-8004
Fax: (202) 208-2106
http://www.ferc.gov/

Senate Liaison:
John Peschke
Congressional Affairs Specialist

Tel: (202) 502-8870

House Liaison:
Jehmal Hudson
Congressional Affairs Specialist

Tel: (202) 502-8004

Department of Health and Human Services

James R. Esquea
Assistant Secretary for Legislation
U.S. Department of Health and Human Services
Hubert Humphrey Building, Room 416 G
200 Independence Avenue, SW
Washington, DC 20201

Congressional Liaison: (202) 690-6786
Human Services: (202) 690-6311
Health Issues: (202) 690-7450
Grants: (202) 690-7094
Fax: (202) 690-7380
http://www.hhs.gov/

Administration on Aging

Brian Lutz
Director of Communication and Consumer Services
Department of Health and Human Services
Administration on Aging
1 Massachusetts Avenue, NW
Washington, DC 20001

Tel: (202) 357-3530
Fax: (202) 357-3555
E-mail: brian.lutz@aoa.hhs.gov

Administration for Children and Families

Scott Logan
Acting Director of Legislation and Regulatory Affairs
Administration for Children and Families
U.S. Department of Health and Human Services
901 D Street, SW
Washington, DC 20447

Tel: (202) 401-4529
Fax: (202) 401-4562
http://www.acf.hhs.gov/

Centers for Disease Control and Prevention

Edward Hunter
Director, Washington Office
Centers for Disease Control and Prevention
395 E Street, SW, Suite 9100
Washington, DC 20201

Tel: (202) 245-0600
Fax: (202) 245-0602
http://www.cdc.gov/

Centers for Medicare and Medicaid Services

Maria Martino
Director of Congressional Affairs
Centers for Medicare and Medicaid Services
Department of Health and Human Services
200 Independence Avenue, SW
Room 337H Humphrey Building
Washington, DC 20201

Tel: (202) 690-8220
Fax: (202) 690-8168
http://www.cms.hhs.gov/default.asp?

This was the Health Care Financing Administration until July 1, 2001.

Food and Drug Administration

Sally Howard
Deputy Commissioner for Policy, Planning, and Legislation
Food and Drug Administration
U.S. Department of Health and Human Services
10903 New Hampshire Avenue
Building 32, Room 2346
Silver Spring, MD 20993

Tel: (301) 796-8900
Fax: (301) 847-8602
http://www.fda.gov/

Health Resources and Services Administration

Leslie Atkinson
Director, Office of Legislation
Parklawn Building, 14C-17
5600 Fishers Lane
Rockville, MD 20857

Tel: (301) 443-1890
Fax: (301) 443-9270
http://www.hrsa.gov

Indian Health Service

Michael Mahsetky
Director of Legislative Affairs
Indian Health Service
801 Thompson Avenue, Suite 400
Rockville, MD 20852

Tel: (301) 443-7261
Fax: (301) 480-3192
E-mail: michael.mahsetky@ihs.gov
http://www.ihs.gov/

National Institutes of Health

Francis Patrick "Pat" White
Associate Director, Office of Legislative Policy and Analysis
National Institutes of Health
U.S. Department of Health and Human Services
Building One, Room 244
Center Drive,
Bethesda, MD 20892

Tel: (301) 496-3471
Fax: (301) 496-0840
E-mail: whitefp@od.nih.gov
http://www.nih.gov/

Substance Abuse and Mental Health Services Administration

Brian Altman
Legislative Director
Substance Abuse and Mental Health Services Administration
U.S. Department of Health and Human Services
1 Choke Cherry Road, Room 8-1053
Rockville, MD 20857

Tel: (240) 276-2009
Fax: (240) 276-2010
E-mail: brian.altman@samhsa.hhs.gov
http://www.samhsa.gov/

Department of Homeland Security

Brian DeVallance
Acting Assistant Secretary for Legislative Affairs
Department of Homeland Security
301 7th Street SW, Mail Stop 0150
Washington, DC 20528-0150

Tel: (202) 447-5890
Fax: (202) 447-5437
http://www.dhs.gov/about-office-legislative-affairs

U.S. Citizenship and Immigration Services

James McCament
Chief, Legislative Affairs
U.S. Citizenship and Immigration Services
20 Massachusetts Avenue, 4th Floor
Washington, DC 20529

Tel: (202) 272-1940
Fax: (202) 272-1955
http://www.uscis.gov/

This bureau handles immigration service functions such as immigrant benefits, adjustment of status to naturalization applications, and requests for asylum and refugee status.

Transportation Security Administration

Sarah Dietch
Assistant Administrator, Office of Legislative Affairs
Transportation Security Administration Headquarters
East Tower, Floor 11, TSA-5
601 South Twelfth Street
Arlington, VA 20598-6001

Tel: (571) 227-2717
Fax: (571) 227-2559
http://www.tsa.gov/public/

U.S. Customs and Border Protection

Michael Yeager
Assistant Commissioner, Office of Congressional Affairs
U.S. Customs and Border Protection
1300 Pennsylvania Avenue, NW
Washington, DC 20229

Tel: (202) 344-1760
Fax: (202) 344-2152
http://www.cbp.gov/

This bureau is the unified border agency in the Department of Homeland Security that manages, controls, and protects the nation's borders at and between official points of entry.

U.S. Immigration and Customs Enforcement

Kathryn Mills
Acting Assistant Director, Office of Congressional Relations
U.S. Immigration and Customs Enforcement
500 12th Street SW, Mail Stop 5003
Washington, DC 20536-5003

Tel: (202) 732-4200
Fax: (202) 732-4269
http://www.ice.gov/index.htm

This bureau focuses on the enforcement of immigration and customs laws within the United States, the protection of specified federal buildings, and air and marine enforcement, including the Federal Air Marshal Service. They perform customs and immigration investigations and collect customs and immigration intelligence.

Federal Emergency Management Agency

Aaron Davis
Director of Legislative Affairs
Federal Emergency Management Agency
500 C Street, SW, Room 714
Washington, DC 20472

Tel: (202) 646-4500
Fax: (202) 646-3600
E-mail: aaron.davis@fema.dhs.gov
http://www.fema.gov/

U.S. Coast Guard

Captain Andy Blomme
Chief, Congressional and Government Affairs Staff
U.S. Coast Guard
470 L'Enfant Plaza East, Room 7110
Washington, DC 20024

Tel: (202) 245-0520
Fax: (202) 245-0529
http://www.uscg.mil/default.asp

For House offices:
Commander Bion Stewart
B-320 Rayburn House Office Building
U.S. House of Representatives
Washington, DC 20515

Capitol ext. 5-4775
Tel: (202) 225-4775
Fax: (202) 426-6081

For Senate offices:
Commander Dan Walsh
183 Russell Senate Office Building
U.S. Senate
Washington, DC 20510

Capitol ext. 4-2913
Tel: (202) 224-2913
Fax: (202) 755-1695

U.S. Secret Service

Faron Paramore
Deputy Assistant Director
Office of Congressional Affairs
U.S. Secret Service
245 Murray Drive, SW, Building T5
Washington, DC 20223

Tel: (202) 406-5676
Fax: (202) 406-5740
http://www.secretservice.gov

Department of Housing and Urban Development

Bernard Fulton
Deputy Assistant Secretary for Congressional Relations
U.S. Department of Housing and Urban Development
451 Seventh Street, SW, Room 10148
Washington, DC 20410-1000

Tel: (202) 708-0380
Fax: (202) 708-3794
http://www.hud.gov

Department of the Interior

Sarah Neimeyer
Director of Congressional and Legislative Affairs
U.S. Department of the Interior
Mail Stop 6242
1849 C Street, NW
Washington, DC 20240-0001

Tel: (202) 208-7693
Fax: (202) 208-5533
http://www.doi.gov

Bureau of Indian Affairs

Darren R. Pete
Director, Office of Congressional and Legislative Affairs
Bureau of Indian Affairs
U.S. Department of the Interior
Mail Stop 3648
1849 C Street, NW
Washington, DC 20240-0001

Tel: (202) 208-5706
Fax: (202) 208-4623
http://www.bia.gov/

Bureau of Land Management

Patrick Wilkinson
Division Chief
Bureau of Land Management
U.S. Department of the Interior
Mail Stop 401-LS
1849 C Street, NW
Washington, DC 20240-0001

Tel: (202) 912-7421
Fax: (202) 245-0050
http://www.blm.gov/nhp/index.htm

Bureau of Ocean Energy Management

Mr. Lee Tilton
Acting Chief, Office of Congressional Affairs
Bureau of Ocean Energy Management
U.S. Department of the Interior
1849 C Street, NW
Washington, DC 20240-0001

Tel: (202) 208-3502
Fax: (202) 208-6048
E-mail: lee.tilton@boem.gov
http://www.boem.gov/

Bureau of Reclamation

Dionne E. Thompson
Chief, Congressional and Legislative Affairs
Bureau of Reclamation
U.S. Department of the Interior
1849 C Street, NW, Room 7545
Washington, DC 20240-0001

Tel: (202) 513-0565
Fax: (202) 513-0304
E-mail: dethompson@usbr.gov
http://www.usbr.gov/

Bureau of Safety and Environmental Enforcement

Julie S. Fleming
Chief, Office of Congressional Affairs
Bureau of Safety and Environmental Enforcement
U.S. Department of the Interior
1849 C Street, NW
Washington, DC 20240-0001

Tel: (202) 208-3827
Fax: (202) 208-3968
E-mail: julie.s.fleming@bsee.gov
http://www.bsee.gov/

Fish and Wildlife Service

Matthew Huggler
Chief, Office of Congressional and Legislative Affairs
U.S. Fish and Wildlife Service
U.S. Department of the Interior
4401 N. Fairfax Dr., Suite 330
Arlington, VA 22203

Tel: (703) 358-2240
Fax: (703) 358-1780
http://www.fws.gov/

National Park Service

Elaine Hackett
Congressional Liaison
National Park Service
U.S. Department of the Interior
1849 C Street, NW, Room 3325
Washington, DC 20240

Tel: (202) 208-7331
Fax: (202) 208-5683
http://www.nps.gov/

Office of Surface Mining Reclamation and Enforcement

Vacant
Congressional Liaison Officer
Office of Surface Mining Reclamation and Enforcement
U.S. Department of the Interior
1951 Constitution Avenue, South Interior
Washington, DC 20240

Tel: (202) 208-2838
Fax: (202) 501-0549
http://www.osmre.gov/

U.S. Geological Survey

Tim West
Congressional Liaison Officer
U.S.G.S. National Center
Room 7A418, Mail Stop 119
12201 Sunrise Valley Drive
Reston, VA 20192

Tel: (703) 648-4455
Fax: (703) 648-5427
E-mail: cong_liaison@usgs.gov
http://www.usgs.gov/

Department of Justice

Peter Kadzik
Deputy Assistant Attorney General, Office
of Legislative Affairs
Office of Legislative Affairs
U.S. Department of Justice
950 Pennsylvania Avenue, NW, Room 1145
Washington, DC 20530

Tel: (202) 514-2141
Fax: (202) 514-4482
http://www.usdoj.gov

Bureau of Alcohol, Tobacco, Firearms and Explosives

John Hageman
Chief, Legislative Affairs Division
Bureau of Alcohol, Tobacco, Firearms and Explosives
U.S. Department of Justice
99 New York Ave, NE
Mail Stop 5.S-144
Washington, DC 20226

Tel: (202) 648-8510
Fax: (202) 648-9708
http://www.atf.gov/

Bureau of Prisons

Jennifer L. Edens
Chief, Office of Legislative Affairs
Federal Bureau of Prisons
U.S. Department of Justice
320 First Street, NW, Room 642
Washington, DC 20534

Tel: (202) 514-9663
Fax: (202) 514-5935
E-mail: jedens@bop.gov
http://www.bop.gov/

Drug Enforcement Administration

Eric Akers
Acting Section Chief of Congressional Affairs
Drug Enforcement Administration
U.S. Department of Justice
8701 Morrissette Drive
Springfield, VA 22152

Tel: (202) 307-7423
Fax: (202) 307-5512
http://www.usdoj.gov/dea/

Federal Bureau of Investigation

Stephen Kelly
Assistant Director of Congressional Affairs
Federal Bureau of Investigation
U.S. Department of Justice
935 Pennsylvania Avenue, NW, Room 7240
Washington, DC 20535-0001

Tel: (202) 324-5051/324-4510
Fax: (202) 324-6490
http://www.fbi.gov/

Office of Justice Programs

Melodee Hanes
Acting Director, Office of Communications
Office of Justice Programs
U.S. Department of Justice
810 Seventh Street, NW, 6th Floor
Washington, DC 20531

Tel: (202) 307-0703
Fax: (202) 514-5958
http://www.ojp.usdoj.gov/

U.S. Marshals Service

Jennifer Eskra
Acting Chief of Congressional Affairs
Office of Congressional Affairs
U.S. Marshals Service
Washington, DC 20530-1000

Tel: (202) 307-9220
Fax: (703) 603-2819
http://www.usdoj.gov/marshals/

Department of Labor

Brian Kennedy
Assistant Secretary for Congressional
and Intergovernmental Affairs
U.S. Department of Labor
200 Constitution Avenue, NW
Washington, DC 20210

Tel: (202) 693-4600
Fax: (202) 693-4642
Correspondence: (202) 693-6100
http://www.dol.gov/

Mine Safety and Health Administration

Carrianna Suiter
Senior Legislative Officer, Office of Congressional Affairs
Mine Safety and Health Administration
U.S. Department of Labor
200 Constitution Avenue, NW
Washington, DC 20210

Tel: (202) 693-4600
Fax: (202) 693-4642
http://www.msha.gov/

Occupational Safety and Health Administration

Laura Delatorre
Senior Legislative Officer
U.S. Department of Labor
200 Constitution Avenue, NW
Washington, DC 20210

Tel: (202) 693-4600
Fax: (202) 693-4642
http://www.osha.gov/

Office of Disability Employment Policy

Jennifer Sheehy
Deputy Assistant Secretary
U.S. Department of Labor
200 Constitution Avenue, NW, Suite S-1303
Washington, DC 20210

Tel: (202) 693-7880
Fax: (202) 693-4929
TTY: (202) 693-4920
http://www.dol.gov/odep/

Department of State

Julia E. Frifield
Assistant Secretary
Bureau of Legislative Affairs
U.S. Department of State
2201 C Street, NW
Washington, DC 20520

Tel: (202) 647-1050
Fax: (202) 647-1618
Correspondence: (202) 647-1608
CongressionalCorrespondence@state.gov
http://www.state.gov

For House Offices:
Lisa Gisvold, Consular Officer
B330 Rayburn House Office Building
U.S. House of Representatives
Washington, DC 20515

Capitol ext. 6-4641
Tel: (202) 226-4641
Fax: (202) 226-4643
E-mail: hill-liaison@state.gov
Visa Inquiries: VisaNet@state.gov
http://www.state.gov/s/h/index.htm

Scott Feeken, Director

Capitol ext. 6-4644
Tel: (202) 226-4644
Fax: (202) 226-4643
E-mail: feekensg@state.gov

For Senate Offices:
Scott Boswell, Consular Officer
189 Russell Senate Office Building
U.S. Senate
Washington, DC 20510

Capitol ext. 8-1605
Tel: (202) 228-1605
Fax: (202) 224-1400
E-mail: hill-liaison@state.gov
Visa Inquiries: VisaNet@state.gov
http://www.state.gov/s/h/index.htm

Marlene Menard, Director

Capitol ext. 8-1603
Tel: (202) 228-1603
Fax: (202) 224-1400
E-mail: menardmm@state.gov

Department of Transportation

Mr. Dana Gresham
Assistant Secretary for Governmental Affairs
U.S. Department of Transportation
1200 New Jersey Avenue, SE
Washington, DC 20590

Tel: (202) 366-4573
Fax: (202) 366-3675/7346
http://www.dot.gov

Federal Aviation Administration

Roderick D. Hall
Assistant Administrator for Government and Industry Affairs
Federal Aviation Administration
800 Independence Avenue, SW, Room 1022
Washington, DC 20591

Tel: (202) 267-3277
Fax: (202) 267-8210
E-mail: roderick.d.hall@faa.gov
http://www.faa.gov/

Department of the Treasury

Alastair M. Fitzpayne
Assistant Secretary for Legislative Affairs
U.S. Department of the Treasury
1500 Pennsylvania Avenue, NW, Room 3134
Washington, DC 20220

Tel: (202) 622-1900
Fax: (202) 622-0534
E-mail: legaffairs@treasury.gov
http://www.ustreas.gov

Bureau of Engraving and Printing

Dawn Haley
Chief, Office of External Relations
Bureau of Engraving and Printing
Fourteenth and C Streets, SW, #107-M
Washington, DC 20228

Tel: (202) 874-3545
Fax: (202) 874-3432
http://www.bep.treas.gov/

Bureau of the Public Debt

Joyce Harris
Director of Legislative and Public Affairs
Bureau of the Public Debt
U.S. Department of the Treasury
401 14th Street, SW
Washington, DC 20227

Tel: (202) 504-3502
Fax: (202) 874-7016
E-mail: joyce.harris@bpd.treas.gov
http://www.publicdebt.treas.gov/

Comptroller of the Currency

Ms. Carrie Moore
Congressional Liaison Director
Comptroller of the Currency
U.S. Department of the Treasury
400 7th Street, SW
Washington, DC 20219

Tel: (202) 649-6440
Fax: (202) 649-5710
E-mail: occ_casework@occ.treas.gov
http://www.occ.treas.gov/

Internal Revenue Service

Leonard Oursler
National Director for Legislative Affairs
Internal Revenue Service
U.S. Department of the Treasury
1111 Constitution Avenue, NW, Room 3241
Washington, DC 20224

Tel: (202) 317-6985
Fax: (202) 317-4250
E-mail: leonard.t.oursler@irs.gov
Correspondence: (202) 317-3700
congressional.correspondence@irs.gov
http://www.irs.gov

U.S. Mint

William Norton
Director of Legislative and
Intergovernmental Affairs
United States Mint
801 Ninth Street, NW
Washington, DC 20220

Tel: (202) 354-7458
Fax: (202) 756-6830

Department of Veterans Affairs

The Honorable Joan Mooney
Assistant Secretary for Congressional and Legislative Affairs
U.S. Department of Veterans Affairs
810 Vermont Avenue, NW
Washington, DC 20420

Tel: (202) 461-6490
Fax: (202) 273-9988
http://www.va.gov

For House offices:
Adam Anicich
Deputy Director, Congressional Liaison Service
B-328 Rayburn House Office Building
U.S. House of Representatives
Washington, DC 20515

Capitol ext. 5-2280
Tel: (202) 225-2280
Fax: (202) 453-5225

For Senate offices:
Adam Anicich
Deputy Director, Congressional Liaison Service
189 Russell Senate Office Building
U.S. Senate
Washington, DC 20510

Capitol ext. 4-5351
Tel: (202) 224-5351
Fax: (202) 453-5218

Independent Agencies, Boards, and Commissions

African Development Foundation

Michele Rivard
Chief of Staff
African Development Foundation
1400 Eye Street, NW, Ste. 1000
Washington, DC 20005-2248

Tel: (202) 673-3916 ext. 179
Fax: (202) 673-3810
http://www.adf.gov/

American Battle Monuments Commission

Christine R. Fant
Director of Finance
American Battle Monuments Commission
Courthouse Plaza 2, Suite 500
2300 Clarendon Boulevard
Arlington, VA 22201

Tel: (703) 696-6323
Tel: (703) 696-6900 (main line)
Fax: (703) 696-6666 (call before faxing)
http://www.abmc.gov/home.php
E-mail: fantc@abmc.gov

Amtrak

Joe McHugh
Vice President, Government Affairs and Corporate
Communications
Amtrak (National Railroad Passenger Corporation)
60 Massachusetts Avenue, NE
Washington, DC 20002

Tel: (202) 906-3867
Fax: (202) 906-3865
http://www.amtrak.com/servlet/ContentServer?
pagename=Amtrak/HomePage

Appalachian Regional Commission

Guy Land
Congressional Liaison
Appalachian Regional Commission
1666 Connecticut Avenue, NW, Room 600
Washington, DC 20009-1068

Tel: (202) 884-7660
Fax: (202) 884-7693
E-mail: gland@arc.gov
http://www.arc.gov/
(Thomas Hunter, Executive Director)

Architectural and Transportation Barriers Compliance Board

Kathy Roy-Johnson
Congressional Liaison
Architectural and Transportation Barriers
Compliance Board
1331 F Street, NW, Suite 1000
Washington, DC 20004-1111

Tel: (202) 272-0041
Fax: (202) 272-0081
TTY: (202) 272-0082
(1-800-993-2822 for technical
assistance on ADA Guide)
E-mail: johnson@access-board.gov
http://www.access-board.gov/

Broadcasting Board of Governors

Suzie Carroll
Congressional Coordinator
Broadcasting Board of Governors
330 Independence Avenue, SW, Room 3360
Washington, DC 20237

Tel: (202) 203-4563
Fax: (202) 203-4568
E-mail: scarroll@bbg.gov
http://www.bbg.gov/

The board has supervised U.S. government civilian international broadcasting, including Voice of America, since
FY2000.

Central Intelligence Agency

Neal Higgins
Director of Congressional Affairs
Central Intelligence Agency
Room 7-C38 OHB
Washington, DC 20505

Tel: (703) 482-4151
Fax: (703) 482-0672
http://www.cia.gov/

Commission of Fine Arts

Thomas Luebke, Secretary
Frederick Lindstrom, Assistant Secretary
Commission of Fine Arts
The National Building Museum
401 F Street, NW, Suite 312
Washington, DC 20001-2728

Tel: (202) 504-2200
Fax: (202) 504-2195
E-mail: staff@cfa.gov
http://www.cfa.gov/

Commodity Futures Trading Commission

John P. Riley
Director of Legislative Affairs, Office of the Chairman
Commodity Futures Trading Commission
3 Lafayette Center
1155 21st Street, NW
Washington, DC 20581

Tel: (202) 418-5383
Fax: (202) 418-5525
E-mail: JRiley@cftc.gov
http://www.cftc.gov/

Corporation for National and Community Service

Kimberly Allman
Director of Government Relations
Corporation for National and Community Service
1201 New York Avenue, NW, 10th Floor
Washington, DC 20525

Tel: (202) 606-6707
Fax: (202) 606-3483
http://www.nationalservice.gov/

Election Assistance Commission

Bryan Whitener
Director, Office of Communications, Clearinghouse, and
Congressional Affairs
U.S. Election Assistance Commission
1201 New York Avenue, Suite 300
Washington, DC 20005

Tel: (202) 566-3118
Toll-free: (866) 747-1471
Fax: (202) 566-3127
http://www.eac.gov/
E-mail: HAVAinfo@eac.gov

Environmental Protection Agency

Laura Vaught
Associate Administrator for Congressional
and Intergovernmental Relations
Environmental Protection Agency
1200 Pennsylvania Avenue, NW, Room 3426 ARN
Washington, DC 20460

Tel: (202) 564-5200
Fax: (202) 501-1519
http://www.epa.gov/

Equal Employment Opportunity Commission

Todd Cox
Director, Office of Communications and Legislative Affairs
Equal Employment Opportunity Commission
131 M Street, NE
Washington, DC 20507

Tel: (202) 663-4191
Fax: (202) 663-4912
http://www.eeoc.gov/index.html

Export-Import Bank of the United States

Stephen Rubright
Vice President, Office of Congressional Affairs
Export-Import Bank of the United States
811 Vermont Avenue, NW, Room 465
Washington, DC 20571

Tel: (202) 565-3230 or 3216
Fax: (202) 565-3236
E-mail: stephen.rubright@exim.gov
http://www.exim.gov/

Fannie Mae

Kristin McGovern
Director of Government and Industry Relations
Fannie Mae
3900 Wisconsin Avenue NW
Washington, DC 20016

Tel: (202) 752-6112
Fax: (240) 699-3555
E-mail: congressional_casework@fanniemae.com
http://www.fanniemae.com/portal/index.html

In 1938, the federal government established Fannie Mae to expand the flow of mortgage money by creating a secondary market. It has been private since 1968.

Farm Credit Administration

Michael A. Stokke
Director, Office of Congressional and
Public Affairs
Farm Credit Administration
1501 Farm Credit Drive, Room 4132
McLean, VA 22102-5090

Tel: (703) 883-4056
Fax: (703) 790-3260
E-mail: info-line@fca.gov
http://www.fca.gov/FCA-HomePage.htm

Federal Citizen Information Center

Walt Dornfried
Congressional Liaison
Federal Citizen Information Center
1800 F Street, NW, Room G142
Washington, DC 20405

Tel: (202) 501-1794
Fax: (202) 501-4281
E-mail: walt.dornfried@gsa.gov
http://publications.usa.gov/USAPubs.php

Federal Communications Commission

Greg Guice
Director, Office of Legislative Affairs
Federal Communications Commission
445 Twelfth Street, SW, Room 8-C445
Washington, DC 20554

Tel: (202) 418-1900
Fax: (202) 418-2806
Correspondence: (202) 418-1900
E-mail: greg.guice@fcc.gov
http://www.fcc.gov/

Federal Deposit Insurance Corporation

Eric Spitler
Director, Office of Legislative Affairs
Federal Deposit Insurance Corporation
550 Seventeenth Street, NW, Room 6076
Washington, DC 20429

Tel: (202) 898-7055
Fax: (202) 898-3745
E-mail: erspitler@fdic.gov
http://www.fdic.gov/

Federal Election Commission

Duane Pugh
Director, Congressional Affairs
Federal Election Commission
999 E Street, NW, Room 943
Washington, DC 20463

Tel: (202) 694-1006
Fax: (202) 219-2338
http://www.fec.gov/

Federal Labor Relations Authority

Sarah Spooner
Executive Director
Office of the Chairman
Federal Labor Relations Authority
1400 K Street, NW
Washington, DC 20424

Tel: (202) 218-7791
Fax: (202) 482-6778
E-mail: sspooner@flra.gov
http://www.flra.gov/

Federal Maritime Commission

Stacey Evans
Legislative Counsel
Federal Maritime Commission
800 North Capitol Street, NW
Washington, DC 20573

Tel: (202) 523-5740
Fax: (202) 523-5738
E-mail: sevans@fmc.gov
http://www.fmc.gov/

Federal Mediation and Conciliation Service

Dawn E. Starr
General Counsel
Federal Mediation and Conciliation Service
2100 K Street, NW
Washington, DC 20427

Tel: (202) 606-5444
Fax: (202) 606-5345
E-mail: dstarr@fmcs.gov
http://www.fmcs.gov/internet/

Federal Reserve System

Linda Robertson
Assistant to the Board for Congressional Liaison
Board of Governors of the Federal Reserve System
Twentieth and Constitution Avenue, NW
Washington, DC 20551

Tel: (202) 452-3456
Fax: (202) 452-2611
http://www.federalreserve.gov/

Consumer Financial Protection Bureau

Lisa Konwinski
Director of Legislative Affairs
Consumer Financial Protection Bureau
1700 G Street, NW
Washington, DC 20552

Tel: (202) 435-7960

For case-related matters:
Consumer Response Congressional Coordination and Response
Team

Tel: (202) 435-9400
To initiate a Consumer Response case:
CFPB_GovtConsumerResponse@cfpb.gov

To request status on an existing case:
CFPB_GovtCaseUpdates@cfpb.gov

Federal Retirement Thrift Investment Board

Kim Weaver
Director, External Affairs
Federal Retirement Thrift Investment Board
77 K Street, NE
Washington, DC 20002

Tel: (202) 942-1641
E-mail: kim.weaver@tsp.gov
http://www.frtib.gov
http://www.tsp.gov

The Federal Retirement Thrift Investment Board is the agency that administers the Thrift Savings Plan.

Federal Trade Commission

Jeanne Bumpus
Director, Office of Congressional Relations
Federal Trade Commission
600 Pennsylvania Avenue, NW, Room 404
Washington, DC 20580

Tel: (202) 326-2195
Fax: (202) 326-3585
Sue Taylor, Correspondence: (202) 326-2671
http://www.ftc.gov/

Freddie Mac

For policy matters:
Barbara Matheson Fox
Vice President, Government Affairs
325 7th Street NW, Suite 500
Washington, DC 20004

Tel: (202) 434-8630
Fax: (202) 434-8626
E-mail: barbara_fox@freddiemac.com
http://www.freddiemac.com

For case-related matters:
Anureta Chahal
Government & Industry Relations

Tel: (202) 434-8638
Fax: (202) 434-8626
E-mail: congressional_inquiries@freddiemac.com

Chartered by Congress in 1970, Freddie Mac is a stockholder-owned corporation that maintains money flow to mortgage lenders in support of home ownership and rental housing.

General Services Administration

Lisa Austin
Associate Administrator, Office of Congressional and
Intergovernmental Affairs
General Services Administration
1800 F Street, NW, Room 6120
Washington, DC 20405

Tel: (202) 501-0563
Fax: (202) 219-5742
E-mail: lisa.austin@gsa.gov
http://www.gsa.gov/portal/category/100000

Institute of Museum and Library Services

Gladstone Payton
Congressional Affairs Officer
Institute of Museum and Library Services
1800 M St. NW, 9th Floor
Washington, DC 20036

Tel: (202) 653-4628
Fax: (202) 653-4600
E-mail: gpayton@imls.gov
Public e-mail: imlsinfo@imls.gov
http://www.imls.gov/

Inter-American Foundation

Paul Zimmerman
General Counsel
Inter-American Foundation
901 North Stuart Street, 10th Floor
Arlington, VA 22203

Tel: (202) 683-7118
E-mail: pzimmerman@iaf.gov
http://www.iaf.gov

Legal Services Corporation

Treefa Aziz
Government Relations Manager
Legal Services Corporation
3333 K Street, NW
Washington, DC 20007

Tel: (202) 295-1614
Fax: (202) 337-6386
E-mail: azizt@lsc.gov
http://www.lsc.gov/

Merit Systems Protection Board

For case-related matters:
Rosalyn Coates
Legislative Counsel
Merit Systems Protection Board
1615 M Street, NW
Washington, DC 20419

Tel: (202) 653-7200
Fax: (202) 653-6203
E-mail: legislativecounsel@mspb.gov
http://www.mspb.gov/

For legislative matters:
Rosalyn Coates
Legislative Counsel
Merit Systems Protection Board
1615 M Street, NW, Room 616
Washington, DC 20419

Tel: (202) 254-4485
Fax: (202) 653-6203
E-mail: rosalyn.coates@mspb.gov

Millennium Challenge Corporation

Nicole Cavino
Legislative Officer
Millennium Challenge Corporation
875 15th Street, NW
Washington, DC 20005

Tel: (202) 521-3852
Fax: (202) 521-3700
E-mail: info@mcc.gov or cavinonc@mcc.gov
http://www.mcc.gov/

The Millennium Challenge Corporation (MCC), created in January 2004, represents a new approach to U.S. foreign development assistance. The MCC only supports poor countries that are committed to growth-promoting governance, health, education, and economic policies. See its website for details.

National Aeronautics and Space Administration

L. Seth Statler
Associate Administrator for Legislative and Intergovernmental Affairs
National Aeronautics and Space Administration
300 E Street, SW, Suite 9J24
Washington, DC 20546

Tel: (202) 358-1055
Fax: (202) 358-2984
http://www.nasa.gov/

National Archives and Records Administration

John Hamilton
Director of Congressional Affairs
National Archives and Records Administration
700 Pennsylvania Avenue, NW
Washington, DC 20408

Tel: (202) 357-5100
Fax: (202) 357-5959
E-mail: john.hamilton@nara.gov
http://www.archives.gov

National Capital Planning Commission

Anne R. Schuyler
General Counsel and Congressional Liaison
National Capital Planning Commission
401 Ninth Street, NW, North Lobby, Suite 500
Washington, DC 20004

Tel: (202) 482-7200
Fax: (202) 482-7272
E-mail: anne.schuyler@ncpc.gov
http://www.ncpc.gov/

National Council on Disability

Anne Sommers
Congressional Liaison
National Council on Disability
1331 F Street NW, Suite 850
Washington, DC 20004

Tel: (202) 272-2004
Fax: (202) 272-2022
TTY: (202) 272-2074
E-mail: asommers@ncd.gov
http://www.ncd.gov/

National Credit Union Administration

Todd M. Harper
Director, Office of Public and Congressional Affairs
National Credit Union Administration
1775 Duke Street
Alexandria, VA 22314-3428

Tel: (703) 518-6330
Fax: (703) 518-6409
E-mail: pacamail@ncua.gov
http://www.ncua.gov/

National Endowment for the Arts

Michael Griffin
Congressional Liaison
National Endowment for the Arts
1100 Pennsylvania Avenue, NW, Room 514
Washington, DC 20506

Tel: (202) 682-5434
Fax: (202) 682-5639
E-mail: griffinm@arts.gov
http://www.arts.gov/

National Endowment for the Humanities

Courtney Chapin
Director of White House and Congressional Affairs
National Endowment for the Humanities
1100 Pennsylvania Avenue, NW, Room 509
Washington, DC 20506

Tel: (202) 606-8239
Fax: (202) 606-8588
http://www.neh.gov/

National Gallery of Art

Delia Scott
Congressional Liaison Officer and Director of Special Projects
National Gallery of Art
2000-B South Club Drive
Landover, MD 20785-3230

Tel: (202) 842-6656
Fax: (202) 789-4577
E-mail: d-scott@nga.gov
http://www.nga.gov

The National Gallery is located on the National Mall between 3rd and 6th Street, at Constitution Avenue, NW, Washington, DC.

National Labor Relations Board

For policy matters:
Celine McNicholas
Special Counsel for Congressional and Intergovernmental Affairs
1099 Fourteenth Street, NW, Room 11600
Washington, DC 20570

Tel: (202) 273-0808
Fax: (202) 273-4270
E-mail: lester.heltzer@nlrb.gov
http://www.nlrb.gov/

For case-related matters:
Celeste Mattina
Deputy General Counsel

Tel: (202) 273-3700

National Mediation Board

Mary Johnson
General Counsel
1301 K Street, NW, Suite 250 East
Washington, DC 20572

Tel: (202) 692-5040
Fax: (202) 692-5085
E-mail: johnson@nmb.gov
http://www.nmb.gov/

National Science Foundation

Judith Gan
Head, Office of Legislative and Public Affairs
National Science Foundation
4201 Wilson Boulevard, Room 1245
Arlington, VA 22230

Tel: (703) 292-8070
Fax: (703) 292-9087
http://www.nsf.gov/

National Transportation Safety Board

Jane Terry
Director of Government Affairs
National Transportation Safety Board
490 L'Enfant Plaza, SW
Washington, DC 20594

Tel: (202) 314-6218
Fax: (240) 752-6344
E-mail: jane.terry@ntsb.gov
http://www.ntsb.gov/index.html

Nuclear Regulatory Commission

Rebecca Schmidt
Director, Office of Congressional Affairs
Nuclear Regulatory Commission
Washington, DC 20555-0001

Tel: (301) 415-1776
Fax: (301) 415-8571
http://www.nrc.gov/

Occupational Safety and Health Review Commission

For case-related matters:
Melik S. Ahmir-Abdul
Public Relations Specialist
Occupational Safety and Health Review Commission
1120 Twentieth Street, NW, 9th Floor
Washington, DC 20036-3457

Tel: (202) 606-5370
Fax: (202) 606-5396
E-mail: sahmir-abdul@oshrc.gov
http://www.oshrc.gov/

For legislative matters:
Richard Huberman
Chief of Staff and Legal Counsel to the Chairman
Occupational Safety and Health Review Commission
1120 Twentieth Street, NW, 9th Floor
Washington, DC 20036-3457

Tel: (202) 606-5723
Fax: (202) 606-5396
E-mail: rhuberman@oshrc.gov
http://www.oshrc.gov/

OSHRC is an agency, independent of OSHA, which adjudicates contested OSHA citations.

Office of Personnel Management

Tania A. Shand
Director, Congressional, Legislative, and Intergovernmental
Affairs
Office of Personnel Management
1900E Street, NW
Washington, DC 20415

Tel: (202) 606-1300
Fax: (202) 606-1344
http://www.opm.gov/

Legislative inquiries and correspondence for Elaine Kaplan, Acting Director of OPM, should be directed above.

For case-related matters:
Joanne Herold, Chief of Constituent Services
Office of Personnel Management
B-332 Rayburn House Office Building
Washington, DC 20515

Capitol ext. 5-4955
Tel: (202) 225-4955
Fax: (202)225-4974

Overseas Private Investment Corporation

James Morrison
Special Assistant, Congressional and Intergovernmental Affairs
Congressional Affairs
Overseas Private Investment Corporation
1100 New York Avenue, NW
Washington, DC 20527-0001

Tel: (202) 336-8400
Fax: (202) 336-7949
E-mail: james.morrison@opic.gov
http://www.opic.gov/

Peace Corps

Kate Beale
Director of Congressional Relations
Peace Corps
1111 20th Street, NW
Washington, DC 20526

Tel: (202) 692-2038
Fax: (202) 692-2101
E-mail: kbeale@peacecorps.gov
http://www.peacecorps.gov/

Pension Benefit Guaranty Corporation

Joshua Gotbaum
Director
Pension Benefit Guaranty Corporation
1200 K Street, NW, 12th Floor
Washington, DC 20005-4026

Tel: (202) 326-4010
Fax: (202) 326-4016
http://www.pbgc.gov/

Postal Regulatory Commission

Ann Fisher
Director of Government Relations
Postal Regulatory Commission
901 New York Avenue, NW, Suite 200
Washington, DC 20001

Tel: (202) 789-6803
Fax: (202) 789-6886
E-mail: ann.fisher@prc.gov
http://www.prc.gov/

President's Council on Fitness, Sports and Nutrition

Russell King
Director of Communications
The President's Council on Physical Fitness, Sports and Nutrition
1101 Wootton Parkway, Suite 560
Rockville, MD 20852

Tel: (240) 276-9567
Fax: (240) 276-9860
(Shellie Pfohl, Executive Director)
http://www.fitness.gov/

Railroad Retirement Board

Margaret Lindsley
Director, Office of Legislative Affairs
Railroad Retirement Board
1310 G Street, NW, Suite 500
Washington, DC 20005-3004

Tel: (202) 272-7742
Fax: (202) 272-7728
E-mail: margaret.lindsley@rrb.gov
http://www.rrb.gov/

Recovery Accountability and Transparency Board

Nancy K. DiPaolo
Chief, Congressional and Intergovernmental Affairs
Recovery Accountability and Transparency Board
1717 Pennsylvania Avenue, NW Suite 700
Washington, DC 20006

Tel: (202) 254-7954
Fax: (202) 254-7956
E-mail: nancy.dipaolo@ratb.gov

Sallie Mae

Timothy Morrison
Senior Vice President of Federal Government Relations
701 Pennsylvania Avenue, NW, Suite 560
Washington, DC 20004

Tel: (202) 969-8001
Fax: (202) 969-8030
http://www.salliemae.com/

Sallie Mae primarily provides federally guaranteed student loans originated under the Federal Family Education Loan Program (FFELP). It began as a government-sponsored enterprise (GSE) called the Student Loan Marketing Association in 1973. Currently, it is a private sector company.

Securities and Exchange Commission

Timothy Henseler
Director of Legislative and Intergovernmental Affairs
Securities and Exchange Commission
100 F Street, NE
Washington, DC 20549-0100

Tel: (202) 551-2010
Fax: (202) 772-9250
http://www.sec.gov/

Selective Service System

Richard S. Flahavan
Associate Director of Public and Intergovernmental Affairs
Selective Service System
1515 Wilson Boulevard
Arlington, VA 22209-2425

Tel: (703) 605-4017
Fax: (703) 605-4106
E-mail: RFlahavan@sss.gov
http://www.sss.gov/

Small Business Administration

Nicholas Coutsos
Assistant Administrator for Congressional
and Legislative Affairs
Small Business Administration
409 Third Street, SW, Suite 7900
Washington, DC 20416-2230

Tel: (202) 205-6700
Fax: (202) 205-7374
http://www.sba.gov/

Smithsonian Institution

Nell Payne
Director, Office of Government Relations
Smithsonian Institution
P.O. Box 37012, MRC019
Washington, DC 20013-7012

Tel: (202) 633-5125
Fax: (202) 786-2274
http://www.si.edu/

Social Security Administration

Robert Forrester
Acting Director, Legislative Research and Congressional
Constituent Relations Staff
Social Security Administration
6401 Security Boulevard
Baltimore, MD 21235-0001

Tel: (410) 965-3930
Fax: (410) 966-5388
http://www.socialsecurity.gov/

Social Security Liaison Office

Latrice Wingo and Sylvia Taylor
Congressional Relations Specialists
Social Security Liaison Office
G3 Lobby One, Rayburn House Office Building
Washington, DC 20515

Tel: Capitol ext. 5-3133
Tel: (202) 225-3133
Fax: Capitol ext. 5-3144
Fax: (202) 225-3144

Surface Transportation Board

Matthew Wallen
Director, Office of Public Assistance, Government Affairs and
Compliance
Surface Transportation Board
395 E Street, SW
Washington, DC 20423-0001

Tel: (202) 245-0231
Fax: (202) 245-0461
http://www.stb.dot.gov/

Refer inquiries to Mary Turek, Congressional Liaison.

Tennessee Valley Authority

Emily Reynolds
Senior Vice President, Government Relations
Tennessee Valley Authority
1 Massachusetts Avenue, NW, Suite 300
Washington, DC 20444-0001

Tel: (202) 898-2999
Fax: (202) 898-2998
http://www.tva.gov/

Trade and Development Agency

Tom Hardy
Director for Congressional Affairs
Trade and Development Agency
1000 Wilson Boulevard, Suite 1600
Arlington, Virginia 22209

Tel: (703) 875-4357
Fax: (703) 875-4009
http://www.ustda.gov/

U.S. Agency for International Development

Barbara Feinstein
Deputy Assistant Administrator for Legislative and Public Affairs
Bureau for Legislative and Public Affairs
U.S. Agency for International Development
Ronald Reagan Building, Suite 610
1300 Pennsylvania Avenue, NW
Washington, DC 20523-6100

Tel: (202) 712-4472
Fax: (202) 216-3035
http://www.usaid.gov/

U.S. Commission on Civil Rights

Lenore Ostrowsky
Acting Public Affairs Unit Chief
U.S. Commission on Civil Rights
1331 Pennsylvania Avenue, NW, Suite 1150
Washington, DC 20425

Tel: (202) 376-7700
Fax: (202) 376-7672
http://www.usccr.gov/

U.S. Consumer Product Safety Commission

Christopher Day
Director of Congressional Relations
U.S. Consumer Product Safety Commission
4330 East-West Highway, Room 817
Bethesda, Maryland 20814

Tel: (301) 504-7660
Fax: (978) 967-2797
E-mail: cday@cpsc.gov
http://www.cpsc.gov/

U.S. International Trade Commission

Joshua Levy
Congressional Relations Officer
U.S. International Trade Commission
500 E Street, SW, Room 716
Washington, DC 20436

Tel: (202) 205-3151
Fax: (202) 205-2139
E-mail: Joshua.levy@usitc.gov
http://www.usitc.gov/

U.S. Postal Service

Vacant
Vice President of Government Relations and Public Policy
475 L'Enfant Plaza, SW, Room 10804
Washington, DC 20260-3500

Tel: (202) 268-2506
Fax: (202) 268-6310
http://www.usps.com/

Government Relations

Sheila Meyers, Manager		(202) 268-2353
Talaya Simpson, Sr. Representative		(202)268-4216
Chatika Copeland	IA, KS, MN, NE, ND, SD	(202) 268-5499
Jeremy Simmons	IL, MI, WI	(202) 268-7839
Timothy Grilo	OH, PA	(202) 268-4387
Shaun Chang	IN, KY, MO, TN, WV	(202) 268-7626
Mary Ann Simpson, Manager	AK	(202) 268-3741
Cathy Pagano, Sr. Representative	AZ, AR, CO, LA, MS, NM, OK, TX, WY	(202) 268-3427
James Cari	CA, OR, WA	(202) 268-6029
David Coleman	AS, GU, HI, ID, MT, NV, MP, UT	(202) 268-3745
Vacant		(202) 268-7217
Scott Slusher, Manager		(202) 268-3229
Linda Gilbert, Sr. Representative		(202) 268-3750
Darrell Donnelly	CT, DE, DC, MD, NJ, RI	(202) 268-6748
Jason Lamote	NC, SC, VA	(202) 268-3743
Lambros Kapoulas	AL, FL, GA	(202) 268-3739
Ekaterina Silina	ME, MA, NH, NY, PR, VT, VI	(202) 268-6027

District of Columbia

John-Paul Hayworth
Manager, Federal Affairs
District of Columbia
1350 Pennsylvania Avenue, NW, Room 512
Washington, DC 20004

Tel: (202) 727-7938
E-mail: john-paul.hayworth@dc.gov
http://www.dc.gov

Author Contact Information

Audrey Celeste Crane-Hirsch
Information Research Specialist
acranehirsch@crs.loc.gov, 7-8826